JOHANN SEBASTIAN BACH

BRANDENBURG CONCERTO No. 2

F major / F-Dur / Fa majeur
BWV 1047

Edited by / Herausgegeben von
Karin Stöckl
in collaboration with / in Zusammenarbeit mit
Johannes Adam, Eberhard Enß,
Frauke Schmitz

D0503892

Ernst Eulenburg Ltd

London · Mainz · Madrid · New York · Paris · Prague · Tokyo · Toronto · Zürich

CONTENTS/INHALT

PREFACE / VORWORT

From August 1717 to April 1723 Johann Sebastian Bach was Kapellmeister and Master of the Royal Chamber Music at the Court of Prince Leopold of Anhalt-Cöthen. Bach expressed his feelings about this post retrospectively in a letter to his longstanding friend Georg Erdmann, written in 1730.[1] One may gather from this letter that for Bach the well-paid post of Kapellmeister obviously carried with it a certain prestige and for that reason he felt it to be a demotion to have to trouble himself with a choirmaster's job. On the other hand Bach's comments make it clear that the working conditions in Cöthen became increasingly difficult with the approaching marriage of Leopold to Friederica Henrietta von Bernburg, which took place at the end of 1721. Bach had in fact, in November 1720, already tried to make a change by applying – though without success – for the vacant post of choirmaster at the Jakobikirche in Hamburg.

In this context the fact that Bach sent selected concertos to Berlin, in a dedicatory manuscript, beautifully prepared as a fair copy in his own hand, for Christian Ludwig, Margrave of Brandenburg, youngest son of the Electoral Prince, has particular significance. According to the requirements of his secular post, Bach composed almost exclusively keyboard works, chamber music and instrumental concertos during his time at Cöthen. So when he dedicates some of his works to an equally secular master it is natural to suppose that

Vom August 1717 bis zum April 1723 war Johann Sebastian Bach am Hofe des Fürsten Leopold von Anhalt-Köthen als Kapellmeister und Direktor der Fürstlichen Kammermusiken tätig. Über diese Anstellung in Köthen äußerte Bach sich rückblickend in einem Brief an seinen langjährigen Freund Georg Erdmann aus dem Jahre 1730[1], aus dem zu entnehmen ist, daß für Bach offenbar die gutdotierte Kapellmeisterstelle mit einem gewissen Ansehen verknüpft war und er es daher als Rückstufung empfand, sich um ein Kantorenamt bemühen zu müssen. Anderseits deuten Bachs Äußerungen darauf hin, daß die Arbeitsbedingungen in Köthen durch die bevorstehende Heirat Leopolds mit Friederica Henrietta von Bernburg, die Ende des Jahres 1721 erfolgte, zunehmend problematisch wurden, und tatsächlich hatte Bach sich bereits im November 1720 mit seiner – allerdings erfolglosen – Bewerbung um die vakante Kantorenstelle an St. Jakobi in Hamburg beruflich zu verändern versucht.

In diesem Zusammenhang erhält Bachs Übersendung von ausgesuchten Konzerten nach Berlin an den Markgrafen Christian Ludwig von Brandenburg, den jüngsten Sohn des Großen Kurfürsten, in einem von der Hand des Komponisten selbst in kalligraphischer Reinschrift verfertigten Widmungsautograph besondere Bedeutung. Den Obliegenheiten seiner weltlichen Anstellung gemäß komponierte Bach in der Köthener Zeit fast ausschließlich Klavierwerke, Kammermusik und Instrumentalkonzerte. Wenn er also einem

---

[1] *Bach-Dokumente*, Bach-Archiv, Leipzig, edited by Werner Neumann and Hans-Joachim Schulze, Vol. I, Kassel [-Leipzig] 1963, No. 23

[1] *Bach-Dokumente* hg. vom Bach-Archiv Leipzig durch Werner Neumann und Hans-Joachim Schulze, Bd. I, Kassel [– Leipzig] 1963, Nr. 23

he would choose them from this repertory.[2] Furthermore, in the text of the inscription (in French) to the Margrave dated 24 March 1721, he makes reference to concrete grounds for the dedication of these *Six Concerts avec plusiers instruments*, named nowadays, after their dedicatee, the 'Brandenburg Concertos': 'A couple of years ago I had the good fortune to be heard by your majesty [...]. Your majesty honoured me with the request that I send you a few of my compositions.'

The circumstances of this performance have been much puzzled over. A coincidental meeting between Bach and the Margrave in Meiningen, of which Christian Ludwig's brother-in-law was Duke, or in Carlsbad during a trip made by Leopold early in 1718 would be possibilities; it is more likely however that Bach met the Margrave in Berlin at the beginning of 1719. Prince Leopold had ordered a harpsichord and instructed Bach to collect the instrument from Berlin – as can be verified from an item for travel expenses in the accounts for 1 March 1719.[3]

The Margrave may well have expressed the desire to hear more of Bach's compositions at the time of this performance. The fact, however, that Bach did not comply with the Margrave's wishes until the sud-

ebenfalls weltlichen Herrn einige seiner Werke dedizierte, so ist es naheliegend, daß er sie aus diesem Repertoire auswählte[2]. Im Widmungstext vom 24. März 1721 an den Markgrafen (in französischer Sprache) bezieht sich Bach zudem auf einen konkreten Anlaß für die Dedikation dieser *Six Concerts avec plusieurs instruments*, die nach ihrem Widmungsträger die heute geläufige Bezeichnung „Brandenburgische Konzerte" tragen: „Vor ein paar Jahren hatte ich das Glück, mich vor Ihrer Königlichen Hoheit hören zu lassen [...] Eure Königliche Hoheit beliebte mich mit dem Auftrag zu ehren, Ihr einige meiner Kompositionen zu senden."

Über die Umstände des hier angesprochenen Vorspiels ist viel gerätselt worden. Eine zufällige Begegnung Bachs mit dem Markgrafen in Meiningen, dessen Herzog der Schwager Christian Ludwigs war, oder in Karlsbad anläßlich einer Reise Leopolds im Frühjahr 1718, wäre denkbar, wahrscheinlicher aber ist, daß Bach den Grafen direkt in Berlin Anfang des Jahres 1719 aufsuchte. Fürst Leopold nämlich hatte in Berlin einen Kielflügel bestellt und beorderte Bach zur Abholung des Instrumentes dorthin, was der Posten der Reisespesen auf der Abrechnung vom 1. 3. 1719 belegt[3].

Wohl mag der Markgraf anläßlich dieses Vorspiels den Wunsch geäußert haben, von Bach weitere Kompositionen zu hören. Der Umstand jedoch, daß Bach erst nach zwei Jahren plötzlich mit der Dedikation

---

[2] It seems plausible, owing to this contractual relationship, to put the date of composition somewhere between 1717 and 1721.

[3] *Bach-Dokumente*, Vol. II, Kassel-Leipzig 1969, No. 95. Whether Bach was already in Berlin at the time the harpsichord was ordered or only went there to collect it is of secondary importance. The unusual French of the opening of the dedication 'une couple d'années' obviously encouraged the view that the reason for the dedication is to be found at least two years earlier.

[2] Aufgrund dieses Anstellungsverhältnisses erscheint es plausibel, die Entstehung der Konzerte in eben den Jahren zwischen 1717 und 1721 anzusetzen.

[3] *Bach-Dokumente* Bd. II, Kassel–Leipzig 1969, Nr. 95. Ob Bach bereits bei der Bestellung des Flügels in Berlin weilte oder erst bei dessen Abholung, erscheint zweitrangig. Offenbar hat hier das ungebräuchliche Französisch des Widmungsbeginnes „une couple d'années" dazu verführt, den Anlaß für die Widmung unbedingt um mehr als zwei Jahre rückdatieren zu wollen.

den dedication of these six concertos two years later makes it much more likely that a secret request was the real reason behind the sending of the scores.[4]

This theory is supported by further observations. As already mentioned, for the enclosures which accompanied his dedicatory manuscript Bach drew on the repertoire of instrumental concertos which he had in all probability composed in and for Cöthen – taking into account, of course, the circumstances in Berlin, with which he must have been familiar both from his journey there and from the lively exchange of musicians which took place between Cöthen and Berlin. He probably hoped to perform the concertos himself in Berlin.[5]

In its six works the score mirrors the whole range of types of concertante ensemble music current at the time: the third and sixth concertos display the characteristics of social music-making most clearly, the second and fourth more the concerto grosso type, and Concertos 1 and 5 in their final autograph form document the development towards the solo concerto. Furthermore, a comparison with the copies, still in existence, of the early versions of Concertos 1, 2 and 3 made by the Bach

dieser sechs Konzerte dem Wunsch des Markgrafen nachkam, deutet viel eher auf eine versteckte Bewerbung als wahren Grund für die Übersendung der Partitur hin[4].

Diese These läßt sich durch weitere Beobachtungen stützen: Wie bereits erwähnt, schöpfte Bach bei der Anlage seiner Widmungshandschrift aus seinem Repertoire von Instrumental-Konzerten, das er aller Wahrscheinlichkeit nach in und für Köthen komponiert hatte, wobei er natürlich die Berliner Verhältnisse berücksichtigt haben dürfte, die er aufgrund seiner Reise dorthin, aber auch aufgrund des regen Musikeraustausches, der zwischen Köthen und Berlin stattfand, genau gekannt haben muß. Er kann also durchaus gehofft haben, die Konzerte in Berlin selbst einmal aufzuführen[5].

Die Partitur spiegelt mit ihren sechs Werken die gesamte Palette damals gängiger Typen konzertanter Ensemblemusik: das 3. und 6. Konzert prägen am ehesten den Charakter von Gemeinschaftsspielmusiken aus, das 2. und 4. mehr den Concerto-grosso-Typus und die Konzerte 1 und 5 dokumentieren in ihrer endgültigen Form im Autograph die Hinwendung zum Solokonzert. Darüber hinaus erweist ein Vergleich mit den noch vorhandenen Abschriften der Frühfassungen der Kon-

---

[4] cf. H.-J. Schulze, 'Johann Sebastian Bachs Konzerte – Fragen der Überlieferung und Chronologie', in *Bach-Studien 6. Beiträge zum Konzertschaffen Johann Sebastian Bachs,* Leipzig 1981, p. 15

[5] There is as much uncertainty over the performability of the works over the date of origin. It appears that the pieces as handed down to Penzel, and thus as they were to be found in Cöthen, were certainly performable there. There is no reliable information about the conditions in Berlin. See Heinz Becker, review of 'Johann Sebastian Bach, Sechs Brandenburgische Konzerte hrsg. von Heinrich Besseler, Neue Bach-Ausgabe, Serie VII, Bd. 2 [...], Kritischer Bericht', in *Die Musikforschung* 1960, pp. 115ff.

[4] vgl. hierzu H.-J. Schulze, *Johann Sebastian Bachs Konzerte – Fragen der Überlieferung und Chronologie,* in: *Bach-Studien 6. Beiträge zum Konzertschaffen Johann Sebastian Bachs,* Leipzig 1981, S. 15

[5] Über die Aufführbarkeit der Werke ist ebenso viel gerätselt worden wie über ihr Entstehungsdatum. Sicher scheint es inzwischen zu sein, daß die Werke so, wie sie von Penzel überliefert wurden und also in Köthen wohl zur Verfügung standen, dort auch aufführbar waren. Über die Berliner Verhältnisse existieren keine verläßlichen Angaben. Vgl. Heinz Becker, Rezension *Johann Sebastian Bach, Sechs Brandenburgische Konzerte, hrsg. von Heinrich Besseler, Neue Bach-Ausgabe, Serie VII, Bd. 2 [...], Kritischer Bericht,* in: *Die Musikforschung* 1960, S. 115 ff.

scholar Christian Friedrich Penzel shortly after Bach's death in Leipzig, and of Concerto No. 5 made by Johann Christoph Altnickol, shows that the diversity of the concerto type was extended in many respects in the writing out of the dedicatory score. Bach enriched the instrumentation by the use of unusual instruments such as the violino piccolo in No. 1 and flauto d'éco in No. 4; he divided the cello part in No. 3 and expanded the cadenzas of the solo instruments in Concerto No. 5. In addition, the treatment of the sequence of movements shows Bach's desire to display his skills to the full – by choosing a two-movement composition for the third piece and by extending the first concerto in the drawing up of the manuscript to a quasi four-movement piece.

Although Bach provides a representative cross-section of his concertos in the dedicatory score, it would be mistaken to think of them in terms of a cycle. We have here merely a collection of pre-existing concertos composed as individual works.

After the death of Margrave Christian Ludwig the dedicatory manuscript came into the possession of the Bach scholar Johann Philipp Kirnberger. He in turn handed the score on to his pupil Princess Amalie of Prussia and it was bequeathed with her library to the Joachimsthalschen Gymnasium. From there the score was finally passed on to the Berlin Staatsbibliothek. It was not published until 1850 when, on the centenary of Bach's death, the Brandenburg Concertos were printed for the first time by C. F. Peters in Leipzig.

Translation Penelope Souster

zerte 1, 2 und 3 durch den Bach-Schüler Christian Friedrich Penzel, die dieser kurz nach Bachs Tod in Leipzig anfertigte, sowie des 5. Konzertes durch Johann Christoph Altnickol, daß die Vielgestaltigkeit der Konzert-Typen in mancher Hinsicht bei der Niederschrift der Widmungspartitur noch erweitert wurde. So bereicherte Bach die Besetzung durch die Verwendung ungebräuchlicher Instrumente wie des *Violino piccolo* im 1. und des *Flauto d'echo* im 4. Konzert, differenzierte den Cellopart im 3. und erweiterte die Kadenz des Soloinstrumentes im 5. Konzert. Außerdem zeigt die Behandlung der Satzfolge Bachs Intention, sein umfassendes Können zur Schau zu stellen, wenn er als drittes Stück eine zweisätzige Komposition auswählt und für die Erstellung des Autographs das 1. Konzert quasi zur Viersätzigkeit erweitert.

Obwohl Bach mit der Widmungspartitur die Darstellung eines repräsentativen Querschnittes durch sein Konzertschaffen gibt, wäre es verfehlt, von einem Zyklus zu sprechen: es handelt sich lediglich um eine Sammlung präexistenter und als Einzelwerke komponierter Konzerte.

Das Widmungsautograph gelangte nach dem Tode des Markgrafen Christian Ludwig in den Besitz des Bach-Schülers Johann Philipp Kirnberger. Dieser wiederum übereignete die Partitur seiner Schülerin Prinzessin Amalie von Preußen, mit deren nachgelassener Bibliothek sie dem Joachimsthalschen Gymnasium ausgehändigt wurde, von wo sie schließlich in den Besitz der Berliner Staatsbibliothek überging. Erst 1850, zu Bachs 100. Todestag, erschienen die *Brandenburgischen Konzerte* beim Verlag C. F. Peters in Leipzig erstmals im Druck.

CONCERTO No. 2, BWV 1047

The Second Brandenburg Concerto, *Concerto 2do à 1 Tromba 1 Fiauto. 1 Hautbois. 1 Violino, concertati, è 2 Violini 1 Viola è Violone in Ripieno / col Violoncello è Basso per il Cembalo*,[6] goes one stage further than the earlier-composed Third Concerto along the path away from a form still centred on the Venetian polychoral style towards the solo concerto of the Vivaldi and Tartini type. Within the set of Brandenburg Concertos, it is the most fully-fledged representative model of the concerto grosso, in which the orchestra and an ensemble comprising several soloists are set against one another.

In contrast with the later Concertos Nos. 4 and 5, however, the solo parts are scarcely individualized. The specific characteristics of the recorder, oboe, trumpet and violin are not taken into account motivically or thematically; all four soloists work with the same material, which is merely adapted slightly to the differing capabilities of the instruments. On the basis of stylistic similarities to other works Besseler fixes the year of composition of the Second Concerto as 1719,[7] a dating which, in the light of recent research findings, must be regarded as very early.[8]

As in many of Handel's concerti grossi, the orchestra and the soloists each present a theme of their own at the beginning of the first movement. Yet we cannot speak of genuine thematic dualism in the Second Brandenburg Concerto, since the 'solo theme' increasingly declines in significance

[6] This is the exact title and indication of scoring in the autograph.
[7] cf. Heinrich Besseler, 'Zur Chronologie der Konzerte J. S. Bachs', in *Festschrift M. Schneider*, Leipzig 1955
[8] cf., for example, Hans-Joachim Schulze, 'J. S. Bach s Konzerte. Fragen der Überlieferung und Chronologie', in *Bach-Studien 6. Beiträge zum Konzertschaffen J. S. Bachs*, Leipzig 1981

KONZERT Nr. 2, BWV 1047

Das zweite *Brandenburgische Konzert, Concerto 2do à 1 Tromba 1 Fiauto. 1 Hautbois. 1 Violino, concertati, è 2 Violini 1 Viola è Violone in Ripieno / col Violoncello è Basso per il Cembalo*[6], geht im Vergleich zum dritten, früher komponierten Konzert einen Schritt weiter auf dem Weg von einer noch eher an der venezianischen Mehrchörigkeit orientierten Form zum Solo-Konzert vom Typ Vivaldis und Tartinis. In der Sammlung der *Brandenburgischen Konzerte* repräsentiert es am ausgeprägtesten das Modell des *Concerto grosso*, in dem sich ein Ensemble aus mehreren Solisten und das Orchester gegenüberstehen.

Im Gegensatz zu den später komponierten Konzerten Nr. 4 und 5 sind die Solostimmen jedoch kaum individualisiert. Der spezifische Charakter von Flöte, Oboe, Trompete und Violine bleibt in Motivik und Thematik unberücksichtigt; alle vier Solisten arbeiten mit dem gleichen Material, lediglich den jeweiligen instrumentalen Möglichkeiten leicht angepaßt. Aus der stilistischen Verwandtschaft mit anderen Werken schließt Besseler auf das Jahr 1719 als Entstehungszeit für das 2. Konzert[7], eine Datierung, die nach neueren Forschungsergebnissen als recht früh angesehen werden muß[8].

Wie in vielen *Concerti grossi* von Händel stellen das Orchester und die Solisten zu Beginn des ersten Satzes jeweils ein eigenes Thema vor. Dennoch kann man im 2. *Brandenburgischen Konzert* nicht von einem echten Themendualismus sprechen, denn das „Solo-Thema" verliert im

[6] so der genaue Titel und die Besetzungsangabe im Autograph
[7] vgl. Heinrich Besseler, *Zur Chronologie der Konzerte J. S. Bachs*, in: *Festschrift M. Schneider*, Leipzig 1955
[8] vgl. hierzu z. B. Hans-Joachim Schulze, *J. S. Bachs Konzerte. Fragen der Überlieferung und Chronologie*, in: *Bach-Studien 6. Beiträge zum Konzertschaffen J. S. Bachs*, Leipzig 1981

in the course of the movement: it always appears unaltered and it is not incorporated into the compositional working, so that its effect is if anything that of an episode. The original 'tutti theme', on the other hand, is also taken up by the soloists and is continually re-worked in playful fashion; in the process the solo quartet gradually assumes control and forces the orchestra into the background. In the third movement the soloists dominate even more strongly than in the first, so that the orchestra here has a purely accompanying function; at no point is it incorporated into the musical working.[9]

The choice of instrument for trumpet and horn parts in Bach's music is frequently a matter of contention. The score and the copies of the parts of the Brandenburg Concertos that were prepared by Penzel contain the indication *Tromba o vero corno da caccia* (trumpet or else hunting horn). A factor in favour of the use of the horn, instead of the trumpet that is most commonly used today, is that F major is the key Bach preferred for horn parts, whereas he never - except in the autograph of the Brandenburg Concertos - expressly called for trumpets in F major.[10] Friedrich Smend maintains, indeed, that Bach composed the *tromba* part for the trumpeter Johann Ludwig Schreiber, but at the same time he mentions the fondness of Prince Leopold of Anhalt-Cöthen for hunting and the sound of the (natural) horn, as well as the fact that horn players were often engaged from other principalities.[11] In any case, since trumpet and horn were often played by the same musician, even the payrolls of the court musicians employed in

Verlauf des Satzes immer mehr an Bedeutung, es tritt stets unverändert auf und wird nicht in die Verarbeitung mit einbezogen, so daß es eher episodenhaft wirkt. Das ursprüngliche „Tutti-Thema" hingegen wird auch von den Solisten aufgegriffen und auf spielerische Weise immer neu verarbeitet; dabei übernimmt das Solistenquartett allmählich die Führung und drängt das Orchester in den Hintergrund. Im dritten Satz dominieren die Solisten noch stärker als im ersten, so daß das Orchester hier reine Begleitfunktion hat, es wird an keiner Stelle in die musikalische Arbeit mit einbezogen[9].

Eine häufig strittige Frage ist die Besetzung der Trompeten- und Hornstimmen in der Musik Bachs. In der Partitur und in den Stimmenabschriften, die Penzel von den *Brandenburgischen Konzerten* anfertigte, findet sich die Anweisung *Tromba o vero corno da caccia* (Trompete oder eher Jagdhorn). Für eine Verwendung des Horns anstelle der heute meist gebräuchlichen Trompete spricht, daß F-Dur die von Bach bevorzugte Tonart für Hornpartien ist, er jedoch - außer im Autograph der *Brandenburgischen Konzerte* - in F-Dur niemals ausdrücklich Trompete vorschrieb[10]. Zwar behauptet Friedrich Smend, die Stimme der *Tromba* habe Bach für den Trompeter Johann Ludwig Schreiber komponiert, im gleichen Zusammenhang erwähnt er jedoch auch die Vorliebe des Fürsten Leopold von Anhalt-Köthen für die Jagd und den Waldhornklang sowie die Tatsache, daß häufig Hornisten von auswärts engagiert wurden[11]. Da außerdem Trompete und Horn häufig vom selben Musiker

[9] cf. Rudolf Gerber, *Bachs Brandenburgische Konzerte. Eine Einführung in ihre formale und geistige Wesensart*, Kassel ²1965, pp. 21ff
[10] cf. the introduction to a broadcast of the Brandenburg Concertos by the BBC, 22 February 1971, quoted in notes accompanying the recording of the Concertos, Philips 6700 045
[11] Friedrich Smend, *Bach in Köthen*, Berlin 1951, pp. 17ff

[9] vgl. Rudolf Gerber, *Bachs Brandenburgische Konzerte. Eine Einführung in ihre formale und geistige Wesensart*, Kassel ²1965, S. 21ff.
[10] vgl. die Einführung zur Sendung der Brandenburgischen Konzerte in der BBC am 22. 2. 1971, zit. nach: Textbeilage zur Aufnahme der Konzerte bei Philips 6700 045.
[11] Friedrich Smend, *Bach in Köthen*, Berlin 1951, S. 17ff.

Cöthen cannot provide conclusive evidence whether or not Bach had originally envisaged a horn in the Second Brandenburg Concerto and whether the scoring indication in the dedicatory copy for the Margrave of Brandenburg therefore perhaps shows only that allowance was being made for performance possibilities in Berlin.

The question of scoring is of interest primarily because the character of the Concerto is changed fundamentally and intrinsically if a horn is used in place of a trumpet in the part in question. Since the part notated in F sounds a fourth higher if played by the trumpet, the radiant trumpet sound dominates the other instruments in the two fast movements, especially the quiet recorder. The horn, on the other hand, transposes a fifth lower and thus fits much more firmly into the solo ensemble.

Editorial Notes

The sources

A Autograph score (dedicatory copy for the Margrave of Brandenburg): Deutsche Staatsbibliothek, East Berlin, Sign. Am.B.78. The second concerto can be found on folios 14ᵛ-26ʳ of the volume.

B Copy of the score in the hand of Christian Friedrich Penzel (1737–1801); the source is not A; violone, violoncello and harpsichord are entered, despite their differences, as *Continuo* on one stave per system: Staatsbibliothek Preussischer Kulturbesitz, West Berlin, Sign. Mus. ms. Bach P 1062.

C Copy of the instrumental parts in the hand of Christian Friedrich Penzel;

gespielt wurden, können auch die Köthener Gehaltslisten der dort angestellten Mitglieder der Hofkapelle keinen sicheren Aufschluß darüber geben, ob Bach im 2. *Brandenburgischen Konzert* ursprünglich ein Horn vorgesehen hatte und die Besetzungsangabe im Widmungsexemplar für den Markgrafen von Brandenburg vielleicht nur eine Rücksichtnahme auf die Berliner Aufführungsmöglichkeiten darstellt.

Interessant ist die Frage der Besetzung vor allem deshalb, weil sich der Charakter des Konzertes grundsätzlich und wesentlich verändert, wenn man in der fraglichen Stimme statt einer Trompete das Horn einsetzt. Da die in F notierte Stimme eine Quarte höher klingt, wenn sie von der Trompete gespielt wird, beherrscht in den beiden schnellen Sätzen der strahlende Trompetenklang die übrigen Instrumente, vor allem die leise Blockflöte. Das Horn dagegen transponiert eine Quinte tiefer und ordnet sich so weitaus stärker in das Solistenensemble ein.

Revisionbericht

Die Quellen

A Autographe Partitur (Widmungsexemplar für den Markgrafen von Brandenburg): Deutsche Staatsbiliothek Berlin-Ost, Sign. Am.B.78. Das zweite Konzert befindet sich auf den Blättern 14ᵛ–26ʳ des Partiturbandes.

B Partiturabschrift von der Hand Christian Friedrich Penzels (1737–1801); die Quelle ist nicht A; Violine, Violoncello und Cembalo sind trotz ihrer Unterschiede als *Continuo* in ein System eingetragen: Staatsbibliothek Preußischer Kulturbesitz Berlin-West, Sign. Mus.ms. Bach P 1062.

C Stimmenabschrift von der Hand Christian Friedrich Penzels; weicht von B

deviates only negligibly from B: Staatsbibliothek Preussischer Kulturbesitz, West Berlin, Sign. Mus. ms. Bach St 637.

D Copy of the score in an unknown hand, second half of the eighteenth century; the source is A: Staatsbibliothek Preussischer Kulturbesitz, West Berlin, Sign. Mus. ms. Bach P 256.

E Copy of the instrumental parts in the hand of Johann August Patzig (1738–1816); the source is D; Staatsbibliothek Preussischer Kulturbesitz, West Berlin, Sign. Mus. ms. Bach St 149.

F Copy of the score in an unknown hand, probably originating *c.* 1830; sources may be taken to be B and C: Staatsbibliothek Preussischer Kulturbesitz, West Berlin, Sign. Mus. ms. Bach P 306.

G Copy of the score in an unknown hand, probably originating *c.* 1825; Staatsbibliothek Preussischer Kulturbesitz, West Berlin, Sign. Mus. ms. Bach P 257.

Some notational corrections which Bach himself made in his dedicatory copy for the Margrave of Brandenburg, and which remain unrevised in other copies (including sources B and C), indicate that A itself derives from a source of earlier date. For the present edition, therefore, apart from the primary source A, the copies made by the prefect of the Thomasschule, Penzel, have assumed particular significance. D, E, F and G, since they are later, dependent sources and are of minor value for textual criticism, have been consulted only for problematical passages.

---

nur unwesentlich ab: Staatsbibliothek Preußischer Kulturbesitz Berlin-West, Sign. Mus.ms. Bach St 637.

D Partiturabschrift von unbekannter Hand aus der zweiten Hälfte des 18. Jahrhunderts; die Quelle ist A: Staatsbibliothek Preußischer Kulturbesitz Berlin-West, Sign. Mus.ms. Bach P 256.

E Stimmenabschrift von der Hand Johann August Patzigs (1738 - 1816); die Quelle ist D: Staatsbibliothek Preußischer Kulturbesitz Berlin-West, Sign. Mus.ms. Bach St 149.

F Partiturabschrift von unbekannter Hand, entstanden wohl um das Jahr 1830; als Quellen dürften B und C gelten: Staatsbibliothek Preußischer Kulturbesitz Berlin-West, Sign. Mus.ms. Bach P 306.

G Partiturabschrift von unbekannter Hand, entstanden wohl um das Jahr 1825: Staatsbibliothek Preußischer Kulturbesitz Berlin-West, Sign. Mus.ms. Bach P 257.

Einige von Bach in seinem Dedikationsexemplar für den Markgrafen von Brandenburg selbst vorgenommene Korrekturen von Noten, die sich in anderen Abschriften – dazu zählen die Quellen B und C – unverbessert finden, lassen darauf schließen, daß auch A auf eine früher zu datierende Quelle zurückgeht. Für die vorliegende Ausgabe kommt daher neben der Hauptquelle A den Abschriften des Thomanerpräfekten Penzel eine besondere Bedeutung zu. D, E, F und G wurden, da sie als spätere, abhängige Quellen von geringerem textkritischen Wert sind, nur bei fraglichen Stellen herangezogen.

Editing principles	Editionsprinzipien
Warning accidentals, set within square brackets, are used only when an altered note appears again in a different octave within a given bar and part.	Warnungsakzidentien, in eckige Klammern gesetzt, stehen nur dann, wenn in gleichem Takt und gleicher Stimme ein alterierter Ton in anderer Oktavlage nochmals erscheint.

Karin Stöckl, Johannes Adam,
Eberhard Enß, Frauke Schmitz
Translation Richard Deveson

Karin Stöckl, Johannes Adam
Eberhard Enß, Frauke Schmitz

Einzelanmerkungen

Satz I

Takt 7 Vla. A, D, E 6.N. b′; nach B, C, F korrigiert zu c′ analog zu T. 117.

40 Vl. II, Vla. A setzt *pp*, was analog zu Vl. I als *più piano* aufzufassen ist.

42, 44, 46 Vl. I/II, Vla. A setzt *pp*, hier gedeutet als *più piano* analog T. 40.

118 Ob. 1.–4. N. A 𝅘𝅥𝅯𝅘𝅥𝅯𝅘𝅥𝅯, B, C 𝅘𝅥𝅯𝅘𝅥𝅯𝅘𝅥𝅯 ; analog Fl., Vl. 𝅘𝅥𝅯𝅘𝅥𝅯𝅘𝅥𝅯.

Satz II

6 Fl. 3.–5. N. in den Quellen 𝅘𝅥𝅮𝅘𝅥𝅮 , während Bogensetzung an den Parallelstellen immer 𝅘𝅥𝅮𝅘𝅥𝅮 war.

12 Ob., Vl. Bogensetzung in A über 3.–5. N. fraglich; Vereinheitlichung zu 𝅘𝅥𝅮𝅘𝅥𝅮 analog der gleichen Phrase z. B. in T. 6.

13 Ob. A 1./2. N. 𝅘𝅥𝅮𝅘𝅥𝅮 Fl., Vl. setzen 𝅘𝅥𝅮𝅘𝅥𝅮

38 Vl. A 3.–5. N. Bogensetzung fraglich, analog der vorgenannten Stellen vereinheitlicht.

44 Vl. A ohne Bogen; analog T. 46/47 und aufgrund der anderen Quellen ergänzt.

Title page from the autograph score
Titelseite des Autographs der Partitur

Dedication from the autograph score
Widmung aus dem Autograph der Partitur

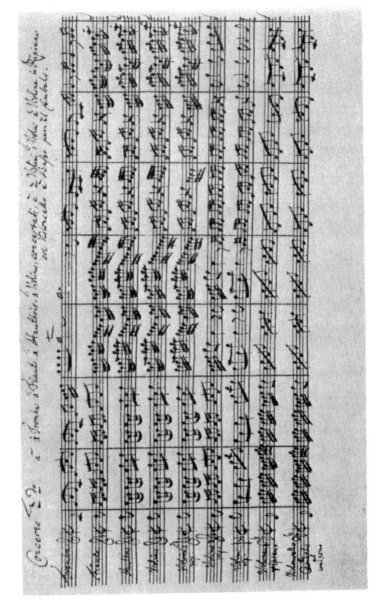

First page from the autograph score of Concerto No. 2
Erste Seite des Autographs zum Konzert Nr. 2

CONCERTO No. 2

Johann Sebastian Bach
(1685–1750)
BWV 1047

Edited by Karin Stöckl
© 1984 Ernst Eulenburg & Co GmbH
and Ernst Eulenburg Ltd

4

6

9

EE 6732

EE 6732

18

tasto solo

accomp.

EE 6732

20

EE 6732

II. Andante

22

III. Allegro assai

32

34

EE 6732